Praise for *Without a Claim*

"The Hebrew word for praise is *yadah,* to give thanks, to extol. Grace Schulman's poetry has always given thanks, but *Without a Claim* is a modern Book of Psalms. Such lush exalting of hickories, white butterflies, dead trumpeters, cursing street talk, painters and their houses, cool jazz, shards, night dancers, whelks, bells, chimes, the color yellow, her father's watches... Indeed, the glory in these radiant sacred songs melds an art of high music with a nuanced love of the world unlike any we've heard before. No matter your mood upon entering this world you'll soon be grateful, and enchanted. 'Let the curator of my life pour my images / out of a basting tube... kindle lightning bugs and luminous / plankton on sand arching to the stars.' In any such house of praise, God herself must be grateful."

   —Philip Schultz, Pulitzer Prize–winning author of *Failure* and
      The God of Loneliness

"*Without a Claim,* Grace Schulman's exhilarating new book of poems, flies free of any restraint or limitation on the imagination. She describes, in poem after poem, what it means to be in the world without a claim: from the Montauk chief who freely traded land for mirrors, with no sense of 'property'—to Miles Davis, leaning like a 'night heron' in the Village—to the author's own balancing act, on 'a circus wire,' above mortal fear and infirmity. These poems, like her ancestors, wander within surmise: 'Ask the sea / at sunrise how a million sparks / can fly over dead bones.' These poems are made of fire and wind, they shimmer in risk, in raw beauty and music. These poems hold no illusions about demarcations and signed-over 'rights'—the permanence they offer lies in the shapes of poetry as pure art, unpossessed."

    —Carol Muske-Dukes, author of the National Book Award finalist
    Sparrow and *Twin Cities*

"Grace Schulman belongs to that small number of lyric poets whose every book expands and deepens the range of the previous one. During the past four decades, she has steadily revisited the themes that preoccupy her: New York City, her Jewish heritage, visual art, concert music, the great jazz artists of the mid-twentieth century, and the sea and shore of Long Island's East End. Seldom has the world been seen so clearly, a vision inseparable from an ethical understanding of experience. She teaches us to answer loss with a greater thing than acceptance: like the Psalmist, like Kaddish, like Rilke, she shows us how to love and praise the world. The post hasn't yet been established, but when it is, Grace Schulman would serve beautifully as New York City's poet laureate."

    —Alfred Corn, author of *Tables*

WITHOUT A CLAIM

BOOKS BY GRACE SCHULMAN

Poetry

Without a Claim
The Broken String
Days of Wonder: New and Selected Poems
The Paintings of Our Lives
For That Day Only
Hemispheres
Burn Down the Icons

Translation

Songs of Cifar: Poems (with Ann McCarthy de Zavala)
    by Pablo Antonio Cuadra
At the Stone of Losses: Poems by T. Carmi

Criticism and Essays

Marianne Moore: The Poetry of Engagement
First Loves and Other Adventures

Editions

The Poems of Marianne Moore (Authorized Edition)
Ezra Pound

WITHOUT A CLAIM

Poems

GRACE SCHULMAN

Mariner Books   A Mariner Original
Houghton Mifflin Harcourt
BOSTON   NEW YORK   2013

For information about permission to reproduce selections from this book, write to Permissions, Houghton Mifflin Harcourt Publishing Company, 215 Park Avenue South, New York, New York 10003.

www.hmhbooks.com

Library of Congress Cataloging-in-Publication Data is available.
ISBN 978-0-544-07377-7

Printed in the United States of America
DOC 10 9 8 7 6 5 4 3 2 1

ACKNOWLEDGMENTS

My thanks to the editors of the following journals in which these poems appeared, often in earlier versions: *Atlantic:* "Antiques Fair," "Celebration," "The Sound." *Cortland Review:* "At the House of Jackson Pollock," "At the Physical Therapist's," "Chauvet," "Danger," "Walking to Elijah." *Hudson Review:* "My Father's Watches," "Division," "Fool's Gold," "Love in the Afternoon," "Hurricane," "Letter Never Sent." *Jewish Quarterly* (London): "Charles Street Psalm." *Kenyon Review:* "Without a Claim," "Moon Shell," "Hickories." *Plume Poetry:* "The Night Dancers," "Bells," "Woman on the Ceiling," "Shadow," "100," "The House on East Eleventh Street." *Southampton Review:* "The Last Crossing," "Whelk." *Warwick Review* (UK): "Havdalah," "Abbaye de Saint-Benoît-sur-Loire," "Handel's Messiah," "The Unbuilder," "The Printmaker." *Yale Review:* "In Praise of Shards." "Celebration" was reprinted in *How We Age: A Doctor's Journey into the Heart of Growing Old* by Marc Agronin, and in *Toward Forgiveness.* "Celebration," "Havdalah," "Moon Shell," and "Without a Claim" were reprinted in the *Alhambra Poetry Calendar.* "Moon Shell" was also reprinted in the *East Hampton Star.*

I'm grateful to Baruch College, CUNY, for a fellowship leave endowing this collection, and for continuing faith and support. My thanks to the John Simon Guggenheim Memorial Foundation, to Yaddo, and to the MacDowell Colony for freedom to pursue the work. For their caring responses to this book in manuscript, I am indebted to Michael Collier, Alfred Corn, Carol Muske-Dukes, Brian Swann, and to my archangels at the press, Nicole Angeloro and Laurence Cooper. Thanks to my assistant, Miriam Lipsius.

To my friends
and *for* Jerry

Those are my best dayes, when I shake with feare.

—John Donne

"Again the sun!
    anew each day; and new and new and new,
    that comes into and steadies my soul."

—Marianne Moore

CONTENTS

I

CELEBRATION

Seeing, in April, hostas unfurl like arias,
and tulips, white cups inscribed with licks of flame,
gaze feverish, grown almost to my waist,
and the oaks raise new leaves for benediction,
I mourn for what does not come back: the movie theater—
reels spinning out vampire bats, last trains,
the arc of Chaplin's cane, the hidden doorways—
struck down for a fast-food store; your rangy stride;
my shawl of hair; my mother's grand piano.
My mother.

                How to make it new,
how to find the gain in it? Ask the sea
at sunrise how a million sparks
can fly over dead bones.

THE SOUND

Accabonac, Shinnecock, Peconic, Napeague,
the creek, the bay, the stream, the Sound, the sounds

of consonants, hard *c*'s and *k*'s. Atlantic,
the ocean's surge, the clicks of waves

collapsed on rocks in corrugated waters,
the crowd circling a stranded whale

sent by the god Moshup to beach at Paumanok.
The Montauks left us names. Their successors,

Millers and Bennetts, whose names are carved
on local gravestones, rode rough tides,

strung trawl lines for cod, and even on Sundays
parked vans by the sea and gazed in fear

until commercial hauls replaced their boats.
Surfmen gave names to streets that bag the tourists

who prize their charm. I hear old sailors rage,
in many languages, against cold winds,

the light now clear, now haze: Pharaohs and Mulfords,
whalers (names unknown), hurl throaty curses

that rise with the sound of waves and with the cries
of an ice-colored gull plucking scallops in shallows.

WITHOUT A CLAIM

Raised like a houseplant on a windowsill
looking out on other windowsills
of a treeless block, I couldn't take it in

when told I owned this land with oaks and maples
scattered like crowds on Sundays, and an underground
strung not with pipes but snaky roots that writhed

when my husband sank a rhododendron,
now flaunting pinks high as an attic window.
This land we call our place was never ours.

If it belonged to anyone, it was
the Montauk chief who traded it for mirrors,
knowing it wasn't his. Not the sailors

who brought the blacksmith iron, nor the farmers
who dried salt hay, nor even the later locals,
whale hunters, the harpooner from Sumatra,

the cook from Borneo, who like my ancestors
wandered from town to port without a claim,
their names inside me though not in the registries.

No more than geese in flight, shadowing the lawn,
cries piercing wind, do we possess these fields,
given the title, never the dominion.

But here we are in April, watching earth rise
with bellflowers that toll, brawl, call, in silence;
daffodils that gleam yellow through sea haze

and cedars at sunrise asking for flame
like a cake with tiers of birthday candles.
Come visit us by shore, up a mud lane.

Duck under the elm's branches, thick with leaves,
on land deeded to us but not to keep,
and take my hand, mine only to give

for a day that shines like corn silk in wind.
We rent, borrow, or share even our bodies,
and never own all that we know and love.

MOON SHELL

August, I walk this shore in search of wholeness
among snapped razor clams and footless quahogs.
How easily my palm cradles a moon shell

coughed up on shore. I stroke the fragments
as, last night, I stroked your arm
smelling of salt, scrubbed clean by the sea air.

Once you loped near me. Now, in my mind's eye,
your rubbery footsoles track sand hills
the shape of waves you no longer straddle.

You inch forward, step, comma, pause,
your silences the wordless rage of pain.
But still at night our bodies merge in sleep

and fit unbroken, like the one perfect shell
I've never found and can only imagine—
and crack when we're apart. I clutch the moon shell,

guardian of unknowing, chipped and silent,
until I fling it down and feel its loss.
Broken, it fit my hand and I was whole.

Antiques Fair

Tents bloom like the circus over things
that serve new purposes: the family hymnal
drowses in a cradle, mugs offer razors,
gifts of an ancestor who isn't yours.

A woman wearing cloudy froth sorts pewter
and holds a blue bottle to the sunlight,
then strokes a gilded mirror for the image
of an 1890s great-grandmother,

young in a tulle gown, plush stole, and tiara.
Sunday, July. In town, the church is empty.
Stark pulpit. Preacher gone. The organist
in a fair booth squinting at tattered sheet music,

"Rejoice, You Pure," the congregation out
picking at fries, bowed over what might read:
Blessed art thou, bald eagle in blond wood,
beak agape, swoop down and clutch us now.

A mother reaches around the baby
strapped on her chest to scoop up beads
marked VINTAGE, *V* for the vast enchanted
who sleepwalk through the fair, lifting tongs

forged by a local smith, as though to salvage
from a great fire icons of a past
flimsy as a chain of paper dolls,
bare as a brass fist with a missing flagpole.

HURRICANE

Warnings go unheard in all this brightness.
Sun's fire licks the poplars on a road
that will be flooded, they say, in three hours.

Abandon homes. Move on, or else you'll spin
with the storm on radar, now an amoeba,
sleeping, one great eye narrowed to an almond,

now a ball of ice tossed in the air,
poised to cast out sharp needles to the ground.
The flagpole trembles on the courthouse roof.

The city gates are closing. Save yourself.
What to believe? On a flat bay, wet wind
washes me clean. Crows are crows, not prophecies.

If so, why does the lightning zigzag closer?
Why are my hands so cold? Because the law
flashes in white letters: *Seek higher ground*.

Why are the people buying Yahrzeit candles
in glass jars, the kind that burn all night?
Because they are the only lights in stores.

Because God, who sends floods, gives us sight,
powerless unpowered. When the marina's
a spectral dock, my body is the only ark

to weather high waves. In screaming darkness,
my neighbor's voice, yesterday a growl,
drifts softly. Now a lamp flickers, now

the storm has passed, the city gates swing open
in a deadly calm. Unpack my fears.
I cannot see the fire in the poplars.

Before the Fall

Guiltless, hearing no sound along the Sound,
biking past slower walkers to the headland,
watching a snowy egret slide down air

and land like a handkerchief on marsh grass,
I never did look down at fallen branches
or cracked clamshells glistening on blacktop,

the way ahead. Then clatter. Crash. And pain's
clearness of vision: stars gleam in daylight
replacing wildflowers a peony blooms

covered with ants, a white hepatica rises
to kiss the sun then droops, its stem cut clean.
X-ray shows white smoke, the malleolus bone,

mallet of a ghost, fogbound, afloat. A stranger
lives inside this mask with slits for eyes,
this boot cast, the leg I thought I owned.

But wait. Think of the flight and not the fall,
not of the bike, the balance lost, the brakes,
the break, the parabolic curve through air.

Think of the rush, the salt, the taste of wind,
the blown hair, bay of sparkling soda water,
starry weeds the locals call bedstraw,

the miracle of all you've never lost.

Variations on a Line by Whitman

Give me the splendid silent juniper,
grown wild on sand, calm in a rage of roses,
where terns dive and pipe-necked cormorants

plunge after whitebait. Give me the splendid
concert hall, hushed until tune-up, the conductor's
first notes, shaping cacophony into order.

Give me the plover's whistle and the soprano's
coloratura Whitman heard when he crunched
shells underfoot and tripped on cobblestones.

Born into bricks-and-glass but near the ocean,
I need them both. Listen promiscuously
to alto, bird, and jackhammer until

boundaries fade: asphalt sand, divine
mechanical, pure impure. Bless the waters
that hurry like the morning rush hour,

praise the audience that chatters
before the Verdi starts, the small talk
lifting my heart like tidewater through stones.

DIVISION

How can I turn from Africa and live?

For DEREK WALCOTT

Contraries bicker here. Even the sun
goes down over the Atlantic's whitecaps
and rises on an unexcited sea;
blood courses in the veins of bougainvillea

and fishbones stalk the coast, reminders of
the drowned. Waves scrawl on sand your double loves,
language of British rule and music of patois
together, like my wishes to recover

the gospel hymn a woman fired at the sea
after the storm, and a muted old-world
prayer. I send this to you as a poet

wrote to Li Po from a street in Warsaw,
in the learned Yiddish of my ancestors,
asking for a poem of praise. And fear.

2

LETTER NEVER SENT

"I always knew in my heart Whitman's mind to be more like my own than any man's living. As he is a very great scoundrel, this is not a pleasant confession."

—Gerard Manley Hopkins

Bawd, savage, unbeliever,
my enemy my brother,
sloucher in the picture

I turn from, wanderer
in and out of the game,
your *heart in hiding,*

your hope flares with the osprey
on serrated wings.
I have learned to say

sassafras, black walnut,
beech, as in your country,
and know as you do

the wren's inscape,
God's mystery stressed,
instressed. You speak

holier than I know
with your *signatures*
and your *handkerchief of the Lord;*

your dogwood, my whitebeam,
the cross that belongs
to neither, and is ours.

How you see the self
inside the ash;
your *Leaves of Grass*

cling like my *Sibyl's Leaves*
blown about her cave,
both as infinite

as the *journeywork of the stars.*
Keep my hayfields. They are yours;
your runs and flourishes, mine.

Let each in his way
catch the hawk alive in air,
tongue-tied, stammering,

in whatever whirled words
will suffice.
I've memorized six of your poems

and must not go further.
The more desirous to read you,
the more determined

I will not,
for my eyes lift to Heaven,
not simply the heavens

of puffed clouds and stars.
Like you I gaze
at masculine trees,

but as you risk
the dangerous beauty
of a boy's bare waist,

I love and fear my love
for the perfect shoulder
of Christ: I see it now,

neck curls, forked beard,
stiff crucified arms
that brought me to Him.

And though I have dreamed
of strolling barefoot
in a green park,

caught my portrait
in a spoon's mirror,
and gazed at Leonardo's bodies,

we cannot walk together,
I in black soutane, you
in an open shirt,

nor can I send this letter,
Jesuit to scoundrel,
unconverted.

Still, in the fire at dawn
and in the sea's whorls,
mind to mind,

God to God,
Walt to Gerard,
I hear your voice.

POETS' WALK, CENTRAL PARK MALL

Shakespeare, Robert Burns, and Fitz-Greene Halleck
sit back in bronze with its metallic claims
to permanence above the passing frolic.

Elm leaves drift from high branches in a panic
of mustard, amber, and pale yellow flame
to shower Shakespeare, Burns, and Fitz-Greene Halleck.

Workers rake leaves that whirl in parabolic
arcs, away and back in greater volume.
Leaves drape lovers in the passing frolic

and wreathe Shakespeare, acting his prince in tragic
grandeur, who declaims, *Had I but time ...*
Oh, I could tell you, Burns and Fitz-Greene Halleck.

Break dancers gyrate to brash hi-fis
as leaves burnish the pasty face of a mime
and redden toddlers in the park's frolic.

Nearby, Cleopatra's Needle rises, phallic,
remembering, like the statues that acclaim
Shakespeare and Burns. But who was Fitz-Greene Halleck?

I've read his bronze unveiling drew historic
top hats, parasols, and mutton sleeves. Time
forgets, but not here. In stark contrast to the frolic,
with Burns and Shakespeare, is Fitz-Greene Halleck.

Street Music, Astor Place

There he is, outside the subway entrance
where sunlit figures race down steps to darkness,
their hearing, like mine, dulled by traffic whines.

He sits low and drums jazz on a plastic box
turned upside down, white with blue letters
stamped by its owner, U.S. POSTAL SERVICE,

made for mail, though with an alto's range.
Now he raises sticks and beats staccato
nonstop, faster than your foot can tap.

Judging from his gaze, the eyes unfocused
—no money jug in sight, no pause for offerings,
no violin cases open like birds' beaks—

I'd say he dives for notes that only he hears,
and swims up proud. He raps sticks soft and loud,
alone, though he may think his rattling joins

a trumpeter's phrases blown at breakneck speed
or a pianist's feathery arpeggios.
For me it does: the sound calls back a cave

of smoke, talk, laughter. A bass player solos.
A tenor sax eases out notes in a whisper
that grows into a regal tone and floats

above the chords. Faces gleam at tables.
But no, the subway-entrance man's alone.
He rumbles on, catching the city's breath,

rolling out solitude in the midst of clatter.
His playing says, if you rub two sticks together
you'll have fire. Or, you might have music.

Woman on the Ceiling

Dura-Europos synagogue, 245 C.E.

Her face shines from the ceiling, ample hair
unbound, the color of wheat in wind,
leaves caught in its stray wisps, her skin paler

than the dark hands of congregants below
reaching to touch the Law on silver scrolls
shouldered and hoisted high from a plaster niche.

She rises shyly, questioning, eyes wide
in this narrow synagogue, the elders
innocent of how the second commandment

will be invoked one day: no graven images.
Who are you, nameless beauty? How you glow
near other bright depictions: a sea monster,

ripe grapes, a lusty goat. To your painter
you might be just another Aphrodite,
topless and seductive, luring celebrants

to the pagan temple down the path,
or a match for saints in the city church
that face front and stare with the same moon eyes.

Your viewers cannot hear the threats, the bans,
the don'ts that came later: don't look up,
don't ever think about the face of Eve

or Adam's thighs in sensuous brushstrokes
on a chapel ceiling. No, keep the law.
You were there all the time, buried in sand,

when artists were artisans, makers of objects,
a silver Kiddush cup, a candelabrum,
unmindful of the breeze twirling your hair.

Now stumbling over rocks in the third century,
the synagogue whole again, just as it was,
I hear the words, *how manifold thy works,*

chanted by congregants whose lifted eyes
see beyond you, through gaps in the wall,
to desert plain, imagining date palms.

You were there all the time, sister of saints
and goddesses, hauled up with shards of a jar,
lost coins, the puzzle of a child's shoe,

a helmet and a sword belt for protection
against attacks, and a gold ring engraved
with only one word, *homonoia*. Unity.

My Father's Watches

Antiques, they tick
for weeks after winding.

When wound they wound me
into wondering

how those faint bells
can tune up when I pass,

and faces stare, wide-eyed,
silver moons tooled with angels,

hunters, and satyrs.
Don't steal my time,

he didn't say, his look rebuking
only himself. He seldom rested

but for the hours
he polished his congregation

of watches, hearing the beat,
gazing at fixed stars.

They kept his days whole
in a blur of motion

even on Sundays at home,
when he brought us smoked fish,

inhaled it like perfume,
and arranged a palette of red-white

slices on a platter,
then combed files of letters

from his parents in Poland,
hoping they were still alive.

Once, while seconds spun,
he listened to a poem

that had come to me slowly.
He glanced at his pocket moon,

and when he turned away
I could see that no words

could mute the drone
of planes in his head.

Watches, give me time
to write lines

my father might hear
over bombs and gunfire.

HAVDALAH

Braided candle, a rainbow of colored wax
twists upward in this sea house. I remember
Saturdays when three stars dotted the sky

candlelight ended Sabbath, red, blue, yellow
casting black silhouettes on plaster walls.
Clutching wine in a silver cup, my father

led us in a chant to praise division
of holy day from weekday, light from shadow.
Sundays my father braided my taffy hair

into one rope over my middy collar
while singing in a half-forgotten Polish,
and now I look at waves and see the basket weavers

of the Montauk people who lived here,
women plaiting swamp grass and flat reeds,
farmers binding wheat, the carder and the twiner,

hand over hand, all workers looking down
at wheat or loom or treebark in the same way.
Tonight, at Sabbath's end, in this seaside town

far from my first house, new faces glow
in the three-color fire of a braided candle,
all of them guests, like me, and the flame

tells me that *havdalah,* meaning separation,
divides only to join. Candle, you light
my hands in altering jade and sapphire,

and braid colors together, silk thread
woven into the billowing fire-red tunic
in Castagno's portrait of a Florentine,

yellow for the luminous medallion
in a Muslim prayer rug, the gold thread
in a carpet hung to warm a castle's walls,

the silver in a chapel's blue-green tapestry,
and here, footprints in sand where fishermen
in wine-red shirts braid ropes tight as your coils.

Charles Street Psalm

Downtown, where towers redden after sunrise,
I heard the singing, more like sobbing, harsh,
broken measures, out of tune, choked sighs,
pour from a brick synagogue set between townhouses,

unadorned and hardly noticeable,
but not unnoticing: one immense window,
unblinking in the sun-on-river glare,
looked back at me coldly as I looked in.

I did not know the words, but I caught tremolos
of praise; thanksgiving, oddly, in lament,
blessings grief undivided. I counted twelve,
but I heard thousands, ancestors whose voices

traveled over theirs, amassed in one
common wail, like wind gusts over seas.
Pesukei d'Zimra, morning praise,
each day a psalm sung now, sung then by exiles

in a past my father blurred with Chardonnay.
He seldom spoke of old world, of horse wagons
that jostled him, in hiding, from the road
where his brother, Jan, was shot, nor of his pack

that held Jan's poems which he declaimed for coins,
a grease-stained photo, newspapers to line
freezing shoes. He told another story:
one morning, after fogbound days on shipboard,

caught in the mystery of what would come,
he saw the harbor. Stream spurted from rock,
garnets in sunlight. He thanked brick towers,
sheltered, as I would be, as *they* would be—

twelve early risers on Charles Street—
where the only soldier-and-rifle shadows
were cast by ginkgo and redbud trees,
where the river exploded only with sunrays,

and where the truck that zigzagged over cobblestones
carried only stacked cartons of milk.
Still, those gravelly, unaccompanied
baritones chanted my father's dread-

and-joy that lurked in his discarded memories.
The past he tucked under damask napkins,
one-room house, dirt road on moonless nights,
comes back to me whole. First breath. Possibilities.

Walking to Elijah

She loomed before me like a prophecy,
wearing a black robe that swept the sand
and a dangling crucifix. I stared until

her eyes beamed under a birdlike crest.
She had observed me through the chapel window,
carrying poppies, a worn map, and a note

with ink-blurred numbers, home of my hosts
for Sabbath dinner, 17 Elijah.
The sun went down, squeezed like a fat stewed peach

too bulky for its jar. It would soon be dark.
Her coarse sleeve grazed my arm as she held torn paper.
"I don't know the address, but we'll walk together.

It's good gymnastics." Gliding in black folds
(I thought she'd fly), she waved the scrap
at a man sipping tea. "There's no such place,"

he barked. "Yes, there must be, she's lost her way,"
my black angel insisted, and he joined us.
Lost. Yesterday a bomb had exploded here,

responding to arrests. Shops closed. And now
the Sabbath, day of rest, its supplications
for peace unheeded. Soon our group was growing

into a procession. Asked for Elijah Street,
passersby shrugged and fell in. One lean man
offered advice in Serbian; at the next corner,

a woman stood sobbing, until, curious,
she crept along. People followed me—
or was I following them? Where were we headed?

We passed a mosque, a church in ruins, a cloister.
Hats were skullcaps, knitted cartwheels, scarves,
a fez, over faces with family features.

Inside a basement window, men at prayer
gazed upward: a black condor? No, the nun.
She hovered, then made for another house

and rang a doorbell, the diners sitting down
to Sabbath wine. Still, no one knew Elijah.
It was late before I reached my friends,

and I don't remember anything else that evening
except a black gown, hats, opinions crackling
in a fire of languages that halted prayer.

3

HICKORIES

Why do I write of hickories, whose boughs
touch other boughs across a slender road,
when our neighbor, Haneen, born in Gaza,

cried that a missile ripped her niece apart
in the family garden? The child's father
found her intestines stuck to a cypress bark

and he, too, perished in the raid. Her mother
wrote to Haneen before the news was out,
"Help me. Take my hand." Why do I rave

of hickories reaching out their crooked fingers?
Because before the fires, the child, Lina,
was dropping almonds into a linen napkin.

Soon she would run to offer them for dinner.
Like Lina, I race to show you hickories,
their nuts shrunken brown globes, soon to fall.

SHADOW

Once in Paris I heard a woman sing
of a day to come so hot that sunrise
would dry the seas, the only sound on earth

a cricket's drone, and on that day,
I search for your heart as I search for shadow.
She sang, looked up at me, coal eyes, pale skin,

and a cool wind poured from the narrow street
into the *cave,* dissolving smoke and talk.
I didn't know the story: at the time

the singer loved a black American,
a trumpeter, both twenty-two. I see them run
down boulevards, hear blues. The dream

ended when he left, she stayed, knowing
that stares and jeers would dog their steps downtown.
While the chanteuse invoked a new Pigalle,

the trumpeter, alone, cursing in street talk,
blew notes of loss, spun out of air and silence.
And why recall it now? Well, on this day

in a hot July, when the sun wilts maples,
when fireworks glare from land's end every night,
starbursts shooting high, dimming the stars,

when only the ocean breathes, and the radio's news
is slaughter, a dead trumpeter cuts in,
playing uptempo, and clears the air.

YELLOW

For CHRIS ALBERTSON

The surprise of it, like sunshot clouds,
the blur of a finch through dark pines,
the suddenness of wheat fields at high noon,

the sherry rose that outgrows its trellis,
the chrome of a Japanese print blazing
in a fisherman's coat painted by Van Gogh,

color of memory, color of angels,
the startling color of his hair, as though
the Danish lakes had washed out all impurities,

not like mine, whose ancestors must have waded
muddier waters. When Chris spoke, I saw North,
fjords and mussel beds on coasts

where he spun a rod fishing for trout.
He told me he left Denmark for the South.
Early, he stirred to jazz LPs, to Bessie's

murmurs he would cross an ocean for.
On trains, on foot, he taped field hollers, blues,
work songs, to cut recordings in New York;

ambushed a tenor sax cleaning a washroom;
amazed a bass who hauled bags at the train;
raised up a blind beggar moaning "Search My Soul"

on a rain-racked guitar. Found Ida Cox,
old, still in good voice, who would record
"Hard, Lord," her bent notes filled with pain

risen in praise. What had brought him there?
Yellow again. Yellow of a wartime childhood.
Yellow stars on badges Denmark's Jews

were forced to wear. The king pinned one on.
Dane citizens. His father. Shadows lifted.
North became South, all colors yellow, yellow.

Handel's Messiah

I've been here before, the hall, the hush,
the wait, the hand, the wand, the promised
birth of God. The question, still unanswered,
why do nations furiously rage together?

Tonight is new, though: violins soar
and leap unhampered by Security
over the traffic lights, teary in rain,
the taxis' rush, the sirens, alleyways

between buildings, the eyeless glitter
of high windows facing west, the headwaiter
breathing deep after diners are gone,
and trumpets fire the mica flecks in pavement.

The government shall be upon his shoulder,
a weighty burden in a year that calls
for a messiah. At the Hallelujah
the audience clatters to its feet in unison

without precisely knowing why, then falls
silent again, including this listener,
the granddaughter of David Freiberger,
and it's all right: Dave, the son of a cantor

on Pike Street, walked uptown to hear *Messiah*,
stood dazzled, and in shul on Shabbat
chanted Hebrew prayers to *every valley*
shall be exalted. Such was his praise.

Now horns acclaim. I don't know if Messiah
has come, will come to save us, or will come
too late to save us, but never mind,
let the bass roar with winds that tell the story.

BELLS

I hear the summer bells, the chimes, the carillon,
the ring of ice cream vans, a bird's high phrases,
church bells that bonged out colors, blue for bridesmaids,

an awning necktie, a rainbow scarf,
a wall clock punctuating my father's silences,
his sister lost, cutting through the toneless

black-white headlines and the radio's spondees
loud as tower bells: *death camps, mass graves.*
At the movies, newsreels dubbed march music

unheard by crowds fleeing in trucks, on foot.
Only a movie, my mother sang,
her voice a cracked bell. *Raids* and *treaties*

clashed in the news I saved to read in bed,
lulled by auguries in broken phrases
that wafted from the next room. *False rumors,*

only a few killed, many will be saved.
My mother's arms, those voices: *steel arms, firearms.*
I listened to reports filtering in,

of planes, oceans away, that shook our walls,
but how to hear their clamor when bells pealed
and my street jangled in full color at noon.

THE LAST CROSSING

It is not me myself I want to forgive
but the girl I was, unquestioning, who strode
up to the ramp hauling a bag of certainties

and boarded the SS *Constitution*
leaving the island's grapevines for her country
where hopes were whispered under shouts of war.

The ship was both protector and diminisher,
city blocks long, each porthole one of hundreds,
and when at last it hurtled through black water

she gazed at a full sky, empty of doubts,
and her heart lifted, even when a storm
tossed the massive hulk, when immigrant women

wrapped in black gauze vomited below.
She never questioned why they left their homes,
remembering her grandfather who spoke

of the new world, not of getting there in steerage.
Instead she touched her passport, sure of flourishing
as the SS *Constitution* could skim whirlpools.

Mornings she balanced on a seesaw deck
and watched, beyond the sun's halo in fog,
the bare landless horizon of the future,

never dreaming of the day she'd read
that the ship, the SS *Constitution*,
which carried her afloat and incorruptible

with its wood and welded steel and white leather,
would sink one day in tow, near Hawaii,
before it could be fired for scrap iron.

AT THE PHYSICAL THERAPIST'S

You strain for balance on a fat blue globe,
hoping to walk steadily again,

to stand up for the Hallelujah chorus,
kick up autumn leaves, scuff sand, trek anywhere.

I'm told to lurk behind the rubbery planet,
crouched to spring if you should quiver and fall.

Pleats of your shirt deepen as you sway
and right yourself again, your shoulders tense,

and you bitch and curse at someone (fate?
the wounding angel?), mourn your lost strides,

squirm in forced stillness. I think of risk,
your risk, and mine as I write this now,

treading a circus wire strung between landings,
eyes fixed on the line ahead, without a pole.

DANGER,

Rat Poison, nailed to a black locust tree,
emerald leaves, honey-yellow blooms.

Touching bark, turning to read, *No Littering,*
No Loitering, I hear chillier warnings:

Don't stay at the ball or you'll lose your prince.
Look back and lose your love to the underworld.

Don't look back, not even to see
if you've watered the roses, locked the door,

or you'll turn to salt, and worse, you will be nameless
like the one we know only as Lot's wife.

And I believe them. Black locusts burn in sunlight,
the fountain surges new, its rainbow shines

expectant, like the surge of faces. Look
and *don't look back,* not at the kids we were,

sliding in rain. Now you step gingerly,
lame but not lost, with your own name,

taking the high risk of this morning,
one hand on your cane, the other open

to catch honey-yellow blossoms falling
just as our shadows fall on this narrow path,

bounded by poisoned grass, and yet
our boundless road up from the underworld.

4

In Praise of Shards

From far away I saw a low curved thing
awash on shore, a corpse, stripped nude and lying

among chipped shells and stones, bone-white at noon,
a woman, one arm outstretched, the other gone,

legs splayed, hacked at the ankle.
But no. Closer, just driftwood, a tall

cedar, branchless, scoured of its stringy bark.
Unlike Aphrodite, leaning in marble,

long fingers lost, hands snapped off over time,
this wood sculpture, carved by an unseen maker

with the turbulent sea for gouge and mallet,
was nameless and *began* with missing parts.

Only the pelvis was intact, skin smooth,
unsplintered by the harsh ride, and hinting

at other wholenesses, inviting me
to imagine the cut extended arm

in prayer, and shape the head to speak or sing.
I came for answers, asking a cracked shell:

Why does the mind reach for completeness
when the fragments are all we have?

My mother's note. I found it in her jewelry case
after she died. "These are real pearls, they . . ."

The rest was blurred. I see her at her table
writing what she could never say without

noticing I had not caught their fire.
The ropes are gone. The image is what stays.

CHAUVET

Raise a torch to flicker on cave walls
and see the horses caught in flight, sleek manes
rising like smoke rings in clear air.
Some dark force lured a nomad
to crawl into a cave with a homemade lamp;

his palette, colors of earth, fire, ash,
charcoal from burned pine, and blood-red ochre
he'd blow through a reed. He scraped the paint
and rubbed out lines until the last horse reared
and the dream took form: imperious stag,

rhino, bison, aurochs, stories on walls.
What drew him there? Not hunger but the hunger,
when winter threatened, nightfall terrified,
the clan slaughtered, to see in blackness
a golden plain. Some say the cave was an altar,

the beasts sacred, but I think the task
was to get it right, the horse's leap,
the fawn's terror, the lion's charge, knowing
that in a life of change those animals
would stay. They have. The ibex glowers.

Horses still snuffle the cave walls,
jaws open in surprise, eyes wide in wonder.
That's where it began, and why I slog
through rank black soil to find radiant images
with horses in high winds to guide my hand.

Love in the Afternoon

Two white butterflies
shimmy over a bed
of tulips, quivering
like a long sentence
waiting
for a main clause.
They kiss and drift apart
and kiss again,
lips open,
deeper this time.

The pair are not mating,
which they will do
back to back on a leaf,
though I cannot imagine
anything that airy
can procreate.
No, they are ballerinas
in a pas de deux
gone improvisational
and free,

moving in rhythm
with one another.
Now they quicken
like thin fingers
unbuttoning a shirt
and twining around
stiff curls

on bare skin,
until, abashed,
face flushed,

holding my breath,
I turn away
from all that radiance.
Later, they flutter
alone,
in smaller arcs,
the vowels high fliers
ungrounded
by consonants,
and sometimes
they flick my ear.

THE VISIT

Thomas Wentworth Higginson and Emily Dickinson

In Amherst one August afternoon,
the heat spell over, a red flush rose

in him when he saw her, shy and simmering by turns,
brandy hair pinned back while the Nouns flowed, unbound.

Quivering, he lifted her tiny hand
and brushed her white sleeve. Spark, hiss, blaze.

The man who managed words in cooler air
had stirred to her art: blooms and snow gusts drifted

in letters he'd read nightly. Now, in daylight,
she jarred him vowing that a poem, if true,

could make her body *so cold no fire*
can warm me. He could never warm that chill,

and though he warmed to her deep thoughts, to glow
was not to burn. This new love wanted nothing

but all, his Soul in Awe. He rose up quickly,
paler now, and promised, *I'll be back sometime,*

meaning never, and stepped to the door.
Later he wished for the grit to risk the danger

of beauty's wounds. Hadn't he charged in battle?
Now mild air stifled him. He wanted thunder

and freezing rain, a *Divine Insanity,*
knowing, at last, *the Danger to be Sane.*

WHELK

Mud-colored outside,
sinuous, shaped
like an overgrown comma,

with gaps that reveal
a spiral inside
like the pearl brooch

my mother kept in velvet
and never wore.
I've read that the whelks

break on the journey
to shore, where they land
among perfect scallops.

I watched this one ravaged
on the road to the headland:
a gull scooped it up,

dropped it to smash the shell,
and with one hoarse shriek
touched down

to gobble its flesh.
I see the ruined shell
as I might gaze

at the headless statues
of gods and imagine
their eyes whole.

For a while
I am a maker
of whelk shells,

carving the curvy pouch,
whittling the crown,
sharpening the tail.

I hold one to my ear
and hear the settlers shout
at the smell of land

and the wreck bell ring
for drowned passengers
washed ashore.

But the shell in my hand,
split open, is mute,
a broken temple

where worshipers once stood,
keeper of what is not said,
and incomplete, as I am

shattered, in doubt,
inside chipped walls,
its silence my silence.

GREEN RIVER

Grave ground can't hold them. They crowd into sight,
elbowing to show you who they were
and what they offer: sea waves in bronze
oddly near a factory plaster angel.

One gravel path connects artists and farmers,
all villagers, no other faith in common:
Jean Stafford speaks knives to Elaine de Kooning
and both lie a few graves from the Bennetts,

my locksmith's family. Frank O'Hara laughs
to see a white paint tube left as a calling card
on Jackson Pollock's boulder. I want to ask them
what the earth gave them when breath failed,

the day they tried to drip more oils,
type more words, or grind another key.
My question would dissolve in wind, the answer
obvious: all work is unfinished

by definition, in brass or on the page,
letters unread, the empty fishing net,
the riderless bike slanted against a tree
on the road to the Green River.

FOOL'S GOLD

Never touch your idols; if you must,
the gilt will rub off on your fingers,
Flaubert warned. My hands sparkling with gold dust,
I brewed espresso, polished tiny saucers,

and watched the gold flecks dance on cups until
they drowned in soapy water. The gilded idol
I'd bought looked down from so high on my bookshelf
I could not see deep scratches where dull metal

peered through, the eyes gone blank behind the stare.
I nudged it and it crashed. My gilt. My guilt,
self-delusion; his, betrayal. Light
from the bay window came in shafts. I swore

that nothing else in life could be so radiant
and stay—trust only the sun to shine again—
while my gold dust flickered and was gone,
like fireflies, like plankton on sand.

ABBAYE DE SAINT-BENOÎT-SUR-LOIRE

For DORE ASHTON

Windows are eyes that see you, see betrayal,
see Saint Benedict's friends poison the cup
that cracked, saving his life. Later, a monk

born Max Jacob, a Jew, wrote words of iron
and air. He prayed here, in this chapel,
psalter in one hand, and in the other

a letter from his friend Jean Cocteau,
about his plea to ask, beg the Gestapo
to save his sister: *If it were you, Max* . . .

The monk, who had heard God's command and hoped
to turn, *convertere,* to a new rule,
lit a slim war-rationed candle on that day,

not for intercession but for friendship's
supreme miracle, which cannot be explained,
just as betrayal can. The monk was arrested

as a Jew, and on the road to Drancy,
where he died, a villager found a letter
never sent, torn, crumpled, flung from a slat

in a prison train. *Cher Jean: Cette fois-ci c'est moi,*
and which, under the abbey's chancel windows,
I hear again: *Dear Jean: This time it's me.*

5

THE NIGHT DANCERS

Praise the shadows that slither up candlelit walls,
that slide out of our bodies, twist and shimmy,
turning red hair, a leaf-print scarf, to gray,

silent partners of talkers at this table,
perhaps demonic selves. Now bouncing high,
now lifting into shallow flight, they never,

unlike their owners, take in food or drink,
but cling, asking only to be remembered
when the flame gutters, when the dawn kills shadow.

While the judge and minister converse
over Merlot in phrases that disguise
bare meanings: *I am the one, the only,*

their slate doubles laugh, vaudeville satirists
and mimickers, knowing the dance will cast
singleness into one shape and one flat darkness.

Bring on the storms, the power outages,
and fetch the lanterns, that we may see ourselves
risen, as they are, dissolved in watery forms,
                              color of muck.

Cool Jazz

Late afternoon, under a salmon sky,
a night heron stalking with charcoal plumage
leaned sideways like a bowling pin off balance

on an island risen for the day
only to sink later with the tide.
I saw Miles Davis lean aslant, a night heron

on Broadway, shoulders hunched, horn pointed down,
until he hoisted brass and played away
sadness of Spain, his sadness, with a tight mute

and without vibrato, making a sound
like moaning underwater, then wider,
embracing all sound, tern cries, wind in cedars.

In the silence of a heron stabbing minnows
you could hear Miles, his hunger of another
kind, deeper, gnawing, harder to feed.

Applause rose up like water slapping the shore.
He lowered his eyes, muttered "Endings just drag me,"
and walked off the platform. The heron flew.

At the House of Jackson Pollock

A woman kneels on grass, blue-green at sunset,
squeezing a basting tube under a hose,
and fire leaps out, the red-orange paint

he dripped on canvas tacked to floorboards.
She is the keeper of his rainbow enamels,
guardian of knives and twigs, washer of bowls

for mixing seashells, sand, and broken glass.
Before he scattered colors to the floor,
he raged at killers in Spain and painted fires

healing and deadly, hidden in yellow ochre.
Outside his house, an egret stalks the shallows,
oaks go about their business, stirring in wind,

a postman carries mail to a lost "resident,"
unaware the rooms crackle with fire.
I want to write my last will by this bay:

Let the curator of my life pour my images
out of a basting tube under a hose,
hang them, backed in wood, at eye level,

and restore my palette of liquid paints
that I may kindle lightning bugs and luminous
plankton on sand arching to the stars.

Tattoo

"When writing, let the object convey feeling,"
a poet said. My student silenced earphones
blaring indie rock, and bared an arm

to show the object: a tattoo. I thought
a wingy angel or a scorpion
or a dragonfly, such as I'd seen

inked in lurid color to the flesh,
and wondered how it might evoke the feeling.
It was a number, 49316,

ice-blue, an upside-down triangle,
his Jewish grandmother's, five digits
branded on her arm when young, a prisoner

at Auschwitz. She survived, lived long,
and died last year. "She sat too still,
wet-kissed a lot, and never was content.

But she stroked my arm where my tattoo is now."
Her name? "Rebecca. Rivka. She said Hashem,
her God, betrayed her." Wait, I thought, her faith

forbids body marks. My reason failed
when I remembered photographs of faces,
nameless, voiceless. Not Rivka, whose cry,

iambic, meaning *I am*—"Survive, survive!"—
pours through her grandson, who never studied
Torah, who, in his death's-head T-shirt,

torn jeans, and Reeboks, danced out to the beat
of "Hold On," jumped the stairs two at a time,
and wrote of a wind-tossed elm. For Rivka Bloom.

GOD BLESS THE CHILD

Billie's high-lows, deep growls, oboe tones,
laughs big with rage held back, like shag clouds
swollen with rain to come, the stretch, the shape

of syllables, the test, the taste, of reasons:
God bless the child that's got his own. His own.
Bless her who sings *I love,* who sold her mouth

before she tried her voice, and sang
to not redeem the past. For breath. *Solitude*
given, never sold, to a nineteen-forties crowd,

war-tired, that sank in it and woke again
with wishes on the moon (cloud-covered, dim,
while she shone). Bless the evenings, let night wait:

heroin, jail, heroin, and the road sign,
DEAD END, black letters in a yellow diamond,
for her, not us. In my house now,

a hornlike woodwind voice more like,
well, wind in woods, raising muted susurrus
of leaves blocks-long, winds that blow for leaf shadows

to dance on whitewashed walls by candlelight,
and might die down if ever she stopped singing.
Praise the wild fawn, a stream of tawny flesh

that leaps out of the woods, and bless the child,
the wild one who fools with time, her notes
falling before, behind the beat. Her own.

For HEDDA STERNE

Her paintings, with their broken triangles
of light diffused, shine above her bed
as she lies there, gazing at darkness.

"Packing to leave," she says, oddly unfazed,
"and death will be a new experience."
Not yet. The best canvas is still unfinished,

black figure changing shape: a bearded sage,
a tower, an oak chest opening on light.
I think of her at work, high on a ladder,

amber hair in a swirl, painting the light
in white-yellow rays, but in one corner,
red for blood on streets of her first country,

black for boots pacing outside her house
where she sketched with burnt matches on paper,
unaware her hand was striking fire.

Her voice cracks like an old Caruso record
that makes me strain to hear it as it was.
She says she is a cloud, soon to evaporate:

I have reached my center, this room my universe.
I dwell on secrets within the ordinary:
this lamp, this table, not mine,

but on loan. They tell me who I am.
And as her words I wish I could help along
fade, and a wall clock bongs the hours,

I marvel at the beauty of incompleteness:
the light resplendent, the glassy angles
of a prism refracting endless moons,

hinting at a world of things unbroken.

The Printmaker

Veronica, *El Greco,*
Museo de Santa Cruz, Toledo

A miracle, or so the legend goes.
She wiped the face and found it printed
on her napkin. But in this painting

her eyes, amazed and watchful, deepening
like half-hidden moons, tell a fuller story.

Look at the napkin she holds proudly, ample,
windblown. Weeks past she'd cut the linen,

soaked it, hung it to dry, took it to Calvary
seeking the highest image for her craft,

following paths imprinted on her mind,
as though sleepwalking, never knowing

what she would find there. Seeing the fall,
she clutched the fabric, pressed it to his forehead

to soothe him, yes, and also to absorb
spit, mire, blood. Later, she unpacked grief,

stretching the cloth across a frame
she'd planed from acacia wood, and watched

the features grow, radiant, in mud,
black flecked with gold. The beauty. It's the eyes

that glow alike—hers, eyes of the One
who became her Lord, eyes of the painter,

who must have known the power that moved her hand,
dirt-stained now, her art the miracle.

The Unbuilder

*In memory of Nick Marzano, renovation carpenter for
the Harvey Theater, Brooklyn Academy of Music, 1987*

Master of chips and peels, of Doric columns
and plaster newly painted to look old,
scrape ivory walls down to historic brick.
It takes a carpenter to scratch and furrow,
a poet's day job. Nights, too, when you learned

you would die of AIDS. The present running out,
only the past lured, iridescent, real.
What better way to rage than to uncreate
the moment, raise a time out of the time,
one noble hour, and catch it alive

flying a magic scaffold to the dome,
to pummel, scar, undo, unbuild
a playhouse, find its glory in decay.
Where Caruso sang and coughed real blood
into a handkerchief, dye the floorboards red.

Smash the wall clock, setting spidery hands
back to when Ellen Terry frowned as Portia.
Nick, whittle arches, free the scent of furs,
unloose in me the woman who clutches satin,
steps out on cobblestones, and hails a horse taxi

that will race over the Brooklyn Bridge.
When you have finished the unfinishing,
stand on stage before a threadbare curtain,
whisper *Oh, I could tell you,* and bow
to an applause you know will never end.

THE HOUSE ON
EAST ELEVENTH STREET

Sunset, winter. Light snuffed out. No twilight,
no second flare, as the woman leans,
rights herself again, and disappears

into the house, its whitewash chipped and peeling
but still ghost-white, boasting that it had shone
among brownstones. Now the house stays dark.

Once windows lighted up at dinners for twelve,
painters with new loves, sole with style.
On high walls, the year's bravura

in oils, in inks, spoke for the wholeness
of art above their makers' fractured lives.
A crystal chandelier shook with her kisses

and with her disregard—*not that disaster*—
flickering like her eyes when she unwrapped
a canvas, sized it up, followed each line,

and said, *It's like the Aztec carvings,*
the sun, the moon, the life, and suddenly
you're old. I call that painting back tonight

while watching hooded windows under a sky
starless and chilly. Soon she will sort
jottings which might either fill pages

or else be scattered in a breeze. A story's end,
perhaps. But wait. Sidling out of shadow,
a man in jeans with a wheeler bag swings open

the wrought-iron gate, climbs broken steps,
stalls, presses the doorbell, lights go on.
New lover? Foreign guest? I don't know yet.

Cancel the ending. The story begins here.

NOTES

WITHOUT A CLAIM

The Montauk chief is Wyandanch, also known as Wyandance and Wyandank. For details about the Montauks here and elsewhere in this book, I am grateful to *The Montauketts of Eastern Long Island*, by John A. Strong; *Men's Lives*, by Ken Robbins and Bill Strachan; and *Hamptons Bohemia*, edited by Constance Denne and Helen Ayers Harrison.

MOON SHELL

This poem is for Pat Strachan.

WOMAN ON THE CEILING

Seen in an exhibit called "Images of Christ," at New York University's Institute for the Study of Ancient Art, in the autumn of 2011.

CHARLES STREET PSALM

This poem is for Philip Schultz and Monica Banks.

SHADOW

Miles Davis and Juliette Gréco.

YELLOW

Chris Albertson arranged recordings for Riverside Records in the early 1960s.

HANDEL'S MESSIAH

The performance of *Messiah* took place at Avery Fisher Hall, December 13, 2011, with Peter Schreier conducting the New York Philharmonic.

THE VISIT

I am indebted to Brenda Wineapple's *White Heat: The Friendship of Emily Dickinson and Thomas Wentworth Higginson*.

GREEN RIVER
Artists and village workers lie in this cemetery, on Accabonac Road, East Hampton, New York.

ABBAYE DE SAINT-BENOÎT-SUR-LOIRE
Dore Ashton, "Cocteau and His Time: An Intellectual Backdrop," in *Jean Cocteau and the French Scene*, edited by Francis Steegmuller, preface by Arthur King Peters (Abbeville Press, 1984). Thinking that Commandant Abetz, a patron of Jean Cocteau, might intervene, Jacob wrote: "Dear Jean: I'm writing this letter with the indulgence of police around me. We will be at Drancy soon, and that's all I have to say. Sacha [Guitry] said, about my sister, 'If it were he I could do something.' This time it's me. Max."

AT THE HOUSE OF JACKSON POLLOCK
An exhibit called "Men of Fire," honoring Pollock's centenary, ran at the Pollock-Krasner Study Center from August 13 to October 27, 2012. The center, which had been the artists' residence, is in Springs, New York. Helen A. Harrison curated the show.

TATTOO
"When writing . . .": attributed to Wei T'ai, an eleventh-century Chinese poet.

GOD BLESS THE CHILD
The poem was written in a startled response to Whitney Bailliet's observation of Billie Holliday, "She was raised in Baltimore, and she was a wild one." Nevertheless, I'm grateful for Bailliet's *Collected Works: A Journal of Jazz, 1954–2001*.

100
Hedda Sterne, a painter claimed by the abstract expressionists and by the first generation of the New York School artists, actually was independent of styles and trends. Her paintings, dominated by light, are simultaneously of earth and unearthly.

THE PRINTMAKER
This poem is for Alfred Corn.